My Favorite Word
Arcane

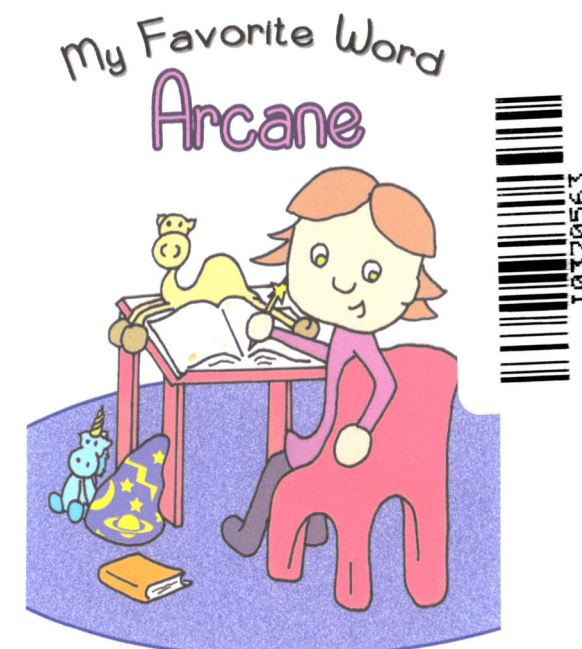

written by Reagan Rothe
illustrated by Dan Weiss

All rights reserved. No part of this book may be reproduced, stored in a retrieval system or transmitted in any form or by any means without the prior written permission of the publishers, except by a reviewer who may quote brief passages in a review to be printed in a newspaper, magazine or journal.

The final approval for this literary material is granted by the author.

First printing

All characters appearing in this work are fictitious. Any resemblance to real persons, living or dead, is purely coincidental.

ISBN: 978-1-944715-10-6
PUBLISHED BY BLACK ROSE WRITING
www.blackrosewriting.com

Printed in the United States of America

My Favorite Word: Arcane is printed in Little Miss Priss

My secret clubhouse is arcane.

You can't get in without saying, "Open Sesame."

Sometimes my friends can be mean to me.

I wish I could use arcane magic to make them nicer.

I hide my favorite toys in an arcane spot.

A place where my little brother can't find them.

I help Dad cook dinner with an arcane recipe.

Half the time, we don't even remember it.

I like playing in the sand.

I even use my shovel to dig for arcane fossils.

My drawings are beautiful to Mom.

She can see the arcane meanings within.

I help clean out the storeroom.

We find all kinds of arcane tools.

I'm writing an arcane story.

One that you should share with all of your friends!

www.ingramcontent.com/pod-product-compliance
Lightning Source LLC
Chambersburg PA
CBHW040121120526
44588CB00027B/8